© 2023 Laura Ann Reed

Published by Sungold Editions
Book design by Chryss Yost

Cover photograph "Winter Night" by Jacob Berghoef.
Used by permission.
Author photograph by Dana Chrysler

ISBN-13: 979-8-9867290-0-8

Shadows Thrown

Poems by

Laura Ann Reed

SUNGOLD EDITIONS • SANTA BARBARA
2023

For Grant Reed
and
In memory of my father,
Emanuel Bickoff
(February 11, 1915 – November 18, 2001)

ACKNOWLEDGEMENTS

Grateful acknowledgement is made to the editors of the following publications in which these works or earlier versions of them previously appeared.

Blue Unicorn: "He Comes Back to Apologize"
Grey Sparrow Journal: "Rain", "His Silence"
MacQueen's Quinterly: "Hell on Wheels", "To a Sister I Didn't Know", "Unspoken", "Inhabited", "Memory Awake"
ONE ART: a Journal of Poetry: "Only Now", "Thief"
Snapdragon: A Journal of Art & Healing: "Among the Elysian Fields"
SWWIM Every Day: "The Sweetness"
The Dillydoun Review: "A Rattling of Broken Bells"
The Loch Raven Review: "Absolution", "Shadows Thrown"
Third Wednesday: "Moth Wings"
Verse-Virtual: "How We Get the Final Word", "The Calculation"
Willawaw Journal: "Red Bird of Love", "No Cats"

Special thanks to James Crews for early encouragement; to Stellasue Lee for subduing my inner critic; to Rebecca Starks for seeing the figure in the stone; to mentor, Laure-Anne Bosselaar for her brilliance and generosity; to Chryss Yost at Sungold Editions for bringing to the process of publication her consummate skill and grace; and to Grant Reed, for everything you are and do that makes this writing life possible.

CONTENTS

To a Sister I Didn't Know

At three, I watched, helpless, as our mother's belly swelled.
I'd lie in bed casting spells, singing hymns of disappearance.
Who could know you'd have curls the shade of ripe apricots,
that your death would feel like accusation, indictment.

I'd lie in bed casting spells, singing hymns of disappearance,
and was later told you only lived a day, less than allotted to a fly.
I didn't know your death would feel like accusation, indictment,
that I'd dream of an orange kitten dying on a cyclone fence.

I was later told you only lived a day, less than allotted to a fly.
I want to say your absence feels like an unopened love letter,
that I dream of an orange kitten dying on a cyclone fence.
Now, from windows, I wave to a neighbor's flame-haired girl.

I want to say your absence feels like an unopened love letter,
that the streaks of fire in our father's beard bring you home.
Now, from windows, I wave to a neighbor's flame-haired girl.
This making safety in the moment. This fishing in air.

How the streaks of fire in our father's beard bring you home.
Who could know you'd have curls the shade of ripe apricots.
This making safety in the moment. This fishing in air.
At three, I watched, helpless, as our mother's belly swelled.

No Cats

after Robert Hayden

On Sunday mornings, my father tiptoes
from the room where my mother sleeps
curled into her womb's secret of losses.
He closes the door, careful not to let it creak.

I follow him into the kitchen where
he spreads old newspapers over the floor.
Sets out tins of polish, a brush
and flannel cloth. Picks up a shoe. Under
his breath he whistles a tune he claims
he listened to on the radio, as a boy—
a happy song, he says. Perhaps
it's because he whistles off-key
that it sounds sad.

What do I know about the sadness
in this house, the disappointments?
The way sun refuses to stipple
the walls? I look down at the reds,

yellows, blues, and greens
in the linoleum, playing a game:
If I find a cat in the pattern, I can
make a wish. But the daubs
are haphazard, there is no pattern.
Every week I look, but
there are never any cats.

Thief

Early spring, I slip through
    a gap in the privet hedge.

The neighbor's apple tree
    quivers with pale frills of silk.

My mother won't hold me
    in her gaze the way

I stand, enchanted
    by this tree. Won't rock me

like I'm cradled in
    rain-soaked winter limbs,

sheltered in July when
    the thinnest membrane

lies between the bark
    and my sun-dark skin.

In fall, that profusion
    of small, hard fruit—

tart, with bitter
    seeds. Yet, I eat

and eat—pretending
    they hold sweetness.

Inhabited

And now, when I summon up
      that hamper in my parents' room,

what do I seek to resurrect if not
      the daydreams I inhabited

in that shadowed space?
      I want them back—

those idle thoughts
      of the duration I could stay

safely hidden, and of how
      good the special silence there.

Good too, those ripe,
      familiar smells

of my parents—their underwear
      co-mingling without shouts or swearing.

I want it back—that proximity
      to my mother's closet, where

at least six shirtwaist dresses
      waited for me to steal

among them and stow my longing
         between plaids and floral patterns.

Finally, like an afterthought—behind
         those coats and crisp white blouses—

that taffeta gown with its rainbow
         sheen I'd never seen her wear,

its cool, deep folds holding the perfume
         of who she'd been before I knew her.

Shadows Thrown

In his death, my father meanders
among the Rose Garden's stone terraces in the Berkeley Hills—
      vast amphitheater of wind and shifting light.

He stops, shades his eyes, squints at the Bay
and at the City beyond, its towers of steel and concrete,
      its windows that glint in the lowering sun.

            (I once floated rose petals
            down Strawberry Creek while
            he played tennis—set after set.)

He prayed he'd fall dead of old age after
acing a serve, his racquet clattering—
      although it didn't happen that way.

He glides by the courts, now, oblivious
to the cyclone fences and nylon nets.
      He gazes instead at shadows

thrown by roses onto the gravel paths,
or slips into the small waterfall
      where Strawberry Creek spills from

a ledge into a bowl of moss-covered rock. Other times,
he peers up at the living sky, hears traces of bright
      laughter from the throat of his child, and quietly

enters the fog that drifts up the hill from the sea,
dissolving in a saline mist that begins to taste of him—
      barely recalling the scent of grief.

He Comes Back To Apologize

Is that you, sweetheart   I've got these ashes
in my eyes   I came back to   they even make
your hair look gray   what I'm trying to say is
   I've thought things through   and
but my thoughts have been so scattered since
I saw you last   I could tell you
where I've been   the morgue   the flames   the sky
      part of me escaped   what remained
was taken out in that   ridiculously expensive boat
and sprinkled in the Bay   under the Golden Gate
   all these jangled angles I've seen things from
      how your mother blamed you for   when did you
get those dark shadows below your lovely eyes
         I know you hoped I'd take a stand   when
she   started in   and I wish I'd
   such a glare from that window   could you pull
the shade   I do see she was   unreasonable
      and   I   there were reasons
for her   unreasonableness   like the six
      who didn't live   you were the lucky one
the point being   she expected you to be all seven
   and when you weren't she   I   I should have
      my throat's so dry   I'm still choking
from that detritus   debris   it's been   what
      twenty years   since I tried to speak   all that
dust from the chimney smoke   you know I think
I hear your mother calling me   I've got to go
oh don't cry   don't cry   don't make your father
sad   whatever happened to   my happy little girl

Among the Elysian Fields

Naptime. There, in my grandparents' room,
in the crib installed for my stay on the farm,
I lay in a drowsy state of bliss—sated
with home-made ice cream and lavish kisses.

They claim you recall nothing before the age
of four. I say, *Rubbish to that!*—like
my grandmother muttered under her breath.

I remember that scent of lilacs wafting
through the window screen, the hot valley
air on my naked skin, those tiny blooms
that rubbed up against the pane—

though it was entirely possible they were
lilac-colored kittens that wanted to come in
and curl into balls under my chin.

I recall the softness of a hand that plucked
my thumb from my mouth as I fell asleep—
that might have been a purple cat's paw.

How We Get the Final Word

These bookshelves of voices pleading to be heard
remind me of my mother who asked before she died
if I'd given any thought to writing.

You express yourself so well, she said, *you really
should.* That shocked me. I'd never had the slightest
chance to express myself with her.

She'd cut me off or finish my sentences and move
to another topic when I'd try to tell her how
I saw the world. But she asked again.

Yes, that's my plan, I said. I kept my answer
brief, so she couldn't interrupt. *Oh, Laura,
that makes me glad.*

A second shock. When was she ever pleased
about the steps I took to create a life apart from her?
What do you intend to write, she asked.

I paused a moment, then said, *My memoirs.*
The room where we were sipping tea filled
with stillness, like the aftermath of earthquakes.

I should have kept to myself my plan to write about
her once she died. I didn't mean to tell her, but I couldn't
hold it back—the fact I'd get the final word.

Memory Awake

Come in, she calls, and I find her
        drinking that bitter tea she steeps

and steeps until the leaves
        disappear into darkness—

the way it was made
        in Odessa. She doesn't speak.

Should I reach across the tablecloth,
        lay my fingers on her sleeve?

After all, she is my grandmother.
        Although she raised a daughter

who won't hold me, who told me
        no one held her on a lap

when she was small. Fidgeting
        in my chair, I stare

at her shaking hands. How
        they cradle a china cup.

This woman who escaped darkness
        with a husband, but no suitcase

of belongings. A woman for whom
    "belonging" is a foreign word.

She sips her tea, takes a hard candy
    from a jar, places it on her tongue.

As if to sweeten
    what she consigns to silence.

A Rattling of Broken Bells

What was it my mother wanted,
        hated me for not giving her?

She willed me all her artwork—
        including that lithograph

she made of me naked, fifteen.
        I watched her make the sketch,

no love in her eyes. There was nothing
        of myself in that misshapen

face, that distorted
        form reclining on a couch.

When she showed me
        the finished lithograph I tried

to hide my wounds. I recall
        the rigid set of her lips

when I failed to praise it. How
        she turned away

when I began to cry. After she died,
        I shrouded the lithograph

in brown paper. Bound it
     with heavy twine. Later,

I gave it to a woman
     moving out of town.

After this, I knew my mother
     could hurt me no further—

though no matter how I wish
     it weren't, this too is pain.

Absolution

When will we get there? I'd say
as my parents' gray Chrysler rolled
over loose stones and weeds in the endless
dirt road that served as driveway. Dust flying
up. Windows open to the melancholy smell
of oranges fallen under trees—sweetness
sinking back into the soil. Those deep, green
shadows my own private Eden. Finally,
the pomegranate tree coming into view,
and the chicken coop—

In the photograph taken on the farmhouse
steps, I gaze at my father's camera, lean
against my grandfather in his worn overalls—
my hand resting on his knee. I seem to edge
away from my grandmother in the ironed
dress she wears for special occasions.
That tight line of hurt on her lips.

There was the reel of family movies turned
to ash in the Oakland firestorm. Before it
burned, I'd watch myself. Six. Seven. Eight
years old. My skinny shape close
to my grandfather's wiry frame. Sidled
away from the soft bulk of my mother's
mother. Me, the eagerly-awaited first

grandchild whose large, dark eyes,
whose middle name, came from her.

Before my nightly bath I'd linger
in the porch swing listening to the crickets,
their insistent hum like some thought
you can't stop thinking. The satin feel
of evening air on my skin, a balm.

His Silence

My grandfather didn't speak
        of fires burning in the streets,

his birthplace torched, corpse-
        filled ditches—all those

lifeless hands that once fingered
        strings of violins or fringes

of a prayer shawl. *Pogrom*
        was a word I never heard

him use. I never heard him say
        his sister's name. Or mention

who'd been left behind,
        failed to make it out in time.

He wouldn't talk about the boat—
        passage or arrival. The cold

ocean of what he wouldn't say—
        I waded in its shallows.

The Calculation

Last night, in the communal
dining room, her father says,
a man who lives on our floor
had his six children
sitting around him at the table
next to ours.

She thinks of her six brothers
and sisters—the four
who never made it out of darkness,
and the two whose breath
turned to air within
a day.

I was so envious,
watching them, he says.

She thinks of her mother—
how she waits each year
for the one who survived
to gift her with seven
birthday bouquets.

Sweetheart, are you there?
he says.

She tries to think of a way
to explain the calculation:
her love for him
multiplied by his for her
divided by his blindness
to her pain equals silence.

Only Now

But I'm not ready, my father says,
        to be taken off the playing field—

and first I bring him shells that hold
        the sea. Then river stones. Then I

bring his favorite recordings
        of Paul Robeson singing spirituals

and lullabies. These make him cry.
        And it's only now, two decades

later, that I see my error: All he needed
        was for me to be with him, to step

closer to his bedside. To allow into my heart
        what flooded his—all that loneliness.

Unspoken

the way my father gestured with his hand, pleaded
with fevered eyes, my father who wanted me to

lift the oxygen mask so he could speak, wanted
to apologize, confide, explain away my mother's

spite, touch my cheek, watch my disappointment in him
fade, the desperation in his eyes as he pointed to the mask,

the interval before I shook my head: how they come
and come, those moments, like crows at dusk—

dark shapes in a sky heavy with impending night, filled
with everything but silence.

Hell on Wheels

Those weren't his exact words,
        but then he didn't grow up under
                her steel thumb—
or slashed by that well-honed tongue.

He could afford to be polite, the man
        who took over her care
                after my therapist advised me
to move out of state.

When we spoke long-distance, he told me
        other residents cringed in terror
                when her motorized three-thousand dollar
wheelchair rocketed in their direction.

He said Mother gazed straight ahead,
        her painter's smock streaming out behind her
                as she raced to the art room. Mother—
ready to crush a toe, gouge a thigh, bash a knee.

Sometimes I see her rolling down a long corridor.
        Despite polio-crippled limbs she flies
                toward whatever version of Paradise
awaits her among brushes, turpentine, and tubes of paint.

Her smock—streaked with vermillion, emerald, topaz, indigo—
        floats about her emaciated frame
                like the wings of some exotic bird of prey
maddened by an unsated hunger.

The Sweetness

My grandfather peels cellophane wrap
from a fresh pack of Camels,
taps one out, lights up,
and blows a perfect orbit above my head.
I rise on my toes and reach
toward a form that blurs
and disappears.

In the windless heat and deep shadow
of a California orange grove,
I suddenly need to know: *Grandpa,*
how long did that boat take
to get here from Odessa? Where
did your sister go? When he gestures
with a weathered hand, I look down
at the sunbaked ground, hoping
for a glimpse of my great-aunt's face.
But all I see is dust, and a dust-choked jimson-weed.

Grandpa, is it true, what my mother says,
that you brought only those Yiddish songs you wrote?
He goes into the house and comes out
carrying a card-table and two folding chairs.
He sets up his chessboard in the green shade
of a citrus tree and darts from chair
to chair, playing against himself.

He doesn't cheat. I watch him
nudge a knight, a queen.
Grandpa, when you were my age,
did you laugh? Did you dance?
He swivels in his seat and plucks
a Valencia orange from a branch behind his back.
He strips the rind with his pocket knife
and hands me a piece of fruit.
I eat it all, meat, pith, seeds—
the way the earth ate my grandfather's life
and his sister's. The way it will eat mine.
Juice streams down my chin. My eyes sting
from the sweetness.

Red Bird of Love

A poem's final line: *All forms,*
the man wrote, tend toward blur,
reminds me of my dad, how
he recedes into dense fog
and rarely
speaks to me anymore.

Although occasionally a phrase
or two come back from that song
he'd sing when he thought no one was listening:
When the red, red robin comes bob, bob, bobbin'
along, there'll be no more sobbin' when he
starts singing his old sweet song—

Truth lies in silence, he'd say
wearing that pensive look as he polished
his work shoes early Sunday mornings
while I'd watch his face, waiting for him
to say something true.

No confusion in those days over truth's
location. Truth was in my skinny legs
that propelled me to the door
when he came back from the laboratory
reeking of test tubes filled with alfalfa juice.
Truth was in his chemist's slender hands
that dropped briefcase and lunch box

to scoop me up. That man who'd rise
in darkness to lure the sun
above the horizon, who later lullabied
me into dreams. When did his shape
begin to blur, his colors fade?
How I miss him, my dad, that
red bird of love.

Rain

In late November my father
        takes me to the circus in San Francisco.

He drives across the bridge
        in steady rain and parks

around the corner from the circus grounds.
        His black umbrella floats

above my head like some great dark
        bird that only wants to shelter me.

In the crowded tent the elephants
        are dancing to a trainer's whip.

The world spins and blurs
        as I push past knees

and clapping hands. Outside, blasts
        of autumn wind lash

the black umbrella until its ribs
        poke through the battered frame.

My father's overcoat flaps around
        his legs like it's trying to fly.

Moth Wings

When are we going home,
　　　　he asks, like a child who's had enough

of the windy beach, the playground
　　　　swings and slide. He's dying

of pneumonia and a failing heart.
　　　　Propped up in bed between

pale green walls he glides in
　　　　and out of delirium. I take

his hand, the skin cool and dry,
　　　　tissue-thin. Near his bed,

a window onto the starless night
　　　　where a tiny moth batters

itself against the pane.
　　　　And my father says,

Sweetheart, when? as if the way
　　　　out or in is glassy and brief—

a wingbeat.

NOTES

In "To a Sister I Didn't Know" the lines, *This making safety in the moment* and *This fishing in air* were taken from "We Manage Best When We Manage Small" by Linda Gregg.

"No Cats" is after "Those Winter Sundays" by Robert Hayden.

In "Memory Awake" the title was taken from *Remorse—Is Memory—Awake* – by Emily Dickinson.

"Only Now" is after "And" by Jim Moore.

In "Red Bird of Love" the line *All forms, the man wrote, tend toward blur* was taken from "I Look Up and Out at the World Through Reading Glasses" by Diane Seuss. The song, "When the Red, Red Robin", refers to a composition of the same name by Harry Woods, released in 1927.

ABOUT THE AUTHOR

A native of the San Francisco Bay Area, Laura Ann Reed received her undergraduate degree in French and Comparative Literature from the University of California, Berkeley before completing master's degree programs in both the Performing Arts and in Clinical Psychology. She was a dancer and dance instructor in the Bay Area prior to her work as a leadership development trainer at the San Francisco headquarters of the United States Environmental Protection Agency. Her work has appeared in numerous anthologies and literary journals. She and her husband live in the Pacific Northwest.